Servant Leader

Pamela Vann

ISBN 979-8-88851-586-0 (Paperback)
ISBN 979-8-88851-587-7 (Digital)

Covenant Books
11661 Hwy 707
Murrells Inlet, SC 29576
www.covenantbooks.com

Devotion Day 1

Birthing a Servant Leader

While carrying me, the country woman from the deep south with a Jerry curl afro and gold teeth had a hard time birthing me out. She had a miscarriage before conceiving me in the womb. My mother, Ora Bell Alexander Vann, was a prophetic woman. I didn't know the meaning of prophetic or the levels of the ministry until about three years ago. As mentioned earlier, we were just good ole country folks. Ms. Alexander, my mother, explained to me that on her vacation, she slipped down a hill, and the baby before me didn't make it. She decided to try again to carry another baby, which was me. From my mother's words, the doctors began trying to birth me out in the delivery room to start the birthing process. During the process, the physicians realized that I was proceeding through the birth canal in the wrong direction. At that point, the physicians had to contact a specialist to help me get delivered the right way to keep me alive and prevent the umbilical cord from stopping my airway.

Servant leaders must realize that having the right specialists to birth you out, whether in the natural or spiritual, will keep you alive. The specialist came down to turn me around in the right direction so I could come out healthy and safe. In the delivery room, my mother was able to give birth to a healthy eight-pound baby girl.

In the spiritual realm, servant leaders chosen by God do not resemble the rest of the servants. The servant leaders chosen by God do not call themselves pastors, evangelists, ministers, deacons, or elders. They prefer the name servant while proceeding to complete the work of God. Birthing a servant leader in the church takes a person whose main focus is serving and not on titles.

As a small child in Millington, Tennessee, I would go to church seven days a week with my uncle and auntie. After the divorce of my parents, we moved to Springfield, Missouri. In the Ozarks, a lady by the name of Deana Young would pick up children from poverty areas and bring them to church. At that point, I was able to see the love and compassion shown by serving people from oppressed populations. Once I reached adulthood, I decided to go into the field of serving the community. I took a position in a hospital environment in Arizona.

I joined a church and decided to serve while giving back to the community. The pastor of the church, Amos L. Lewis, operated with excellence and gave me the opportunity to serve at his church. In this environment, I signed up to be on the prayer team. As a small child in poverty, I understood the power of prayer when that was the only option to make ends meet. It was a miracle by God. I enjoyed going to church and serving in God's presence.

Many changes began to happen in the atmosphere, so I took my family to a different church without praying about it. At the other church, I experienced very strong spiritual warfare while serving as a greeter. The church would hold secret meetings without inviting everyone on the team. A prophet came to church and prophesied to me as a chosen vessel of God. He stated that God had chosen me at a very young age and that someone in my family had spoken witchcraft over me at the age of six. Servant leaders are targeted at a very young age by word curses or any other spiritual or physical hurt not destined by God. The leaders in the current church refused to come into agreement with the prophecy because I was not a pastor or elder. In addition, I did not look like everyone else who was supposedly chosen by God. All the people speaking in the church were married and had healthy financial support.

I continued to serve as God had told me while at the church. After several years, I was told by the Holy Spirit to go back to the previous church, Rising Star Baptist Church, in Tucson, Arizona. While being at the church for a couple of months, I was notified as being a servant of God, and every person could not carry servants chosen by God, no matter their title.

Servants chosen by God must be carried and delivered by servants chosen by God. Many are called, but few are chosen. Servant leaders must become mindful when being rejected by church leaders, so-called chosen by God. They have been called by God but not chosen to deliver you (servant leader).

As a servant leader, please do not fret or get upset when a leader rejects you. The leader in the church who has rejected you has saved your spiritual birth. The leader in the church who rejected you was a blessing. That leader who rejected you placed the servant leader in place to be chosen by God. The opportunity for the wrong leader to birth you would have taken you out spiritually before you could have been birthed out as a servant leader the right way. The wrong servant leadership team will birth you and take you out. Why would a servant leader birth anyone and then try to take them out? It is a spirit of deception from the enemy. The enemy has servants working on the leadership team in the church, not just chosen vessels selected by God.

Devotion Day 2

The Mother of a Servant Leader's Profile

Ora Bell Alexander, had four siblings and lived with her mother until she was ten years old when her mother passed away. She was sent to live with my uncle Jack and my auntie Ina Mae. She went from being the baby of the family to being selected as the oldest member of the family. Ora would have to cook, clean, and get her young siblings, who were her nieces and nephews, ready for school. She would have to take the responsibility for things that didn't the right way because my aunt had many challenges of her own. Servant leaders have been labeled with mental health diagnoses because of the burden of being chosen by God. Many servant leaders are tasked with many responsibilities during their childhood and serve as adults.

At seventeen, she left the parents who raised her to get married to my father. She was a military wife and a mother of two beautiful daughters. Ora would cook, clean, and take care of her beautiful children. It was explained to me that my oldest sister, Tracy, was very sick at birth. She would have to stay at the hospital because of a breathing condition. Tracy would have to be placed in a bubble to keep her safe from germs and any communicable diseases in the hospital. My paternal grandmother (Saing Lee Vann) and auntie (Ina Mae

Alexander) would pray for Tracy all day and night. Also, Tracy, being a servant leader chosen by God, would tell stories of having dreams while lying in a bubble.

While going through a divorce, my mother got engaged to the father of her baby boy, the youngest of the family. Our youngest sibling was conceived while Ora was on birth control. My brother stayed in the hospital for several months because of complications and side effects from birth control. He became stable enough to go home. Ora gave special attention to the baby of the family. Ora experienced several complications with all of her children. The mother of a servant leader experiences many challenges while giving birth to a servant leader.

Ora decided to move her family from Memphis, Tennessee, to Springfield, Missouri. While in Springfield, Ora was designated as the mother to all the oppressed children in the apartment complex. One sunny day, Ora decided to go put some groceries in the refrigerator of a single mother in the apartment complex. On that same day, the school came to the home to assess the mother's environment for safety without Ora knowing the family's home situation. My mother was contacted by the mother to whom she had delivered the groceries earlier that day. The mother informed Ora that the school was going to make a call to the authorities to take her children away that day after looking in her refrigerator. She asked my mother, "How did you know to come put groceries in my home that day?"

Ora told the lady, "I didn't know. The Holy Spirit told me."

The lady thanked Ora over, over, over, and over again for being able to keep her children who are now adults.

Devotion Day 3

A Servant Leader Experiences Many Dreams and Visions throughout Their Journey

As a small child, I would have dreams like I was looking through my mother's eyes. She would be bending down in a cotton field. After several years of having the same dream, I asked my mother about the dream while in high school. She told me that one day, after getting into an altercation with a neighbor, the neighbor became very upset with her while she was pregnant with me and went to get a shotgun. My mother told me she was hiding in a field so the neighbor would not take her out or her unborn child, which was me. I had the dream of my mother hiding in the field before I was born. God knew a servant leader before they were born in the womb. Also, the devil knew the servant leader before they were born in the womb. It is the reason the devil tried to take out the servant leader as a child and at birth.

While serving in the church as a greeter, I had a vision of a lot of lights with people in white robes, praising God. I didn't think anything about the vision. A week later, I took some time from work and stayed in the house. I started getting hungry, so I went to a not-very-popular grocery store. While looking for a watermelon in the store, I turned into the corner and saw statues of angels. The statues were in different sizes—small, medium, and large—in a regular grocery store. I thought to myself, *This seems very odd.*

I continued to get my items and sat in my car, talking to God. The Holy Spirit told me to drive down the street in the opposite direction from the store. I drove down the street and saw a store called Illumination. In the store, I saw so many lights shining throughout the store. Again, I didn't think anything about it. The Holy Spirit told me to go into a small hole in the wall of the thrift store. I drove around the thrift store several times. I was afraid to go into the store because I could not see anything there, and God was speaking to me very loudly to go inside. I decided to go into the store and look around. I decided to walk out and leave. While leaving the store, I looked down and saw a statue that looked like Jesus's head, holding two tablets. On this day, I was able to visualize the vision God was trying to show me that day—greeting outside the church.

One night, I had a dream about my mother crying. I went to church on Wednesday night for Bible study. The leader of the worship service prayed for deliverance for all the people in the church. At the time, the leader decided to have a lady come up to the front for deliverance. In Sunday school, that particular lady discussed about going to a previous church that was a cult. When she came up to the front for deliverance prayer, I heard the Holy Spirit say, "Move out of the way." Politely, I went to the back of the church and moved from the front position. The lady started crawling on the floor in the church and walking in the direction where I had stood before she came to the front. She kept scanning the room like she was looking for something. I decided to stand behind another lady in the church. It appeared the lady was unable to find what she was looking for, and the worship leader asked her to go back and sit down. I understand that evil spirits in the church set out to look for servant leaders. My mother was trying to warn me that the church service was the reason she was crying in my dream.

About three years ago, I kept having a dream of myself sitting on a bridge, waiting to come into a warehouse. I asked many leaders what that dream mean. The leaders told me, "Oh, it just explains you going into some type of ministry." There was so much water in my dream. I never did tell anyone close to me about the dream. Once I arrived on the East Coast, I was met with a lot of water in my new city. I kept saying, "I see now that this is what the dream was about, with me living around all this water on the East Coast."

One day, I decided to get up and travel to a different part of the city. While traveling, I was able to cross the bridge that had all the water in my dream. I got concerned because I didn't see the warehouse on the bridge. After a couple of weeks, I got a chance to look around a new area close to a local university. I was able to find the warehouse in my dream. Many leaders in the church have put this dream in the category of some type of prophecy.

Until the age of four, I was raised by both of my parents in Millington, Tennessee, on a naval base. The area of Millington, Tennessee, has cotton fields farther than the eyes can reach. It is mapped with the work of God and beauty. When I turned five, my mother and father went through a rocky divorce. My mother continued to let me stay with close family members, Uncle Jack and Auntie Ina Mae. Yes, the names Jack and Ina Mae set the tone for very country names. My uncle and auntie were good ole kinfolk who worked to become the best servants for our family.

Devotion Day 4

God Will Call Servant Leaders to Operate in an Unfamiliar Land

One day, I decided to accept work on the West Coast. While traveling to work, the Holy Spirit had me continue to pray while driving twenty-four hours from the Midwest to the West Coast. Once I reached El Paso, Texas, it was raining very heavily, mixed with hail, in conjunction with a rainbow. During my time in the car praying, I crossed a bridge that did not have any railings. The rain was pouring hard, and my cell phone had lost reception. Without being able to see through the hail, the Holy Spirit was able to guide me across the bridge. It was through the power of prayer that the wind didn't pick up my tiny car to cross over the bridge. The Holy Spirit protects servant leaders when the enemy causes a heavy storm, whether in the natural or in the spirit.

Finally, I arrived at my location on the West Coast. I had to learn a lot of new things while moving to a new location. On the job, I was in situations where I dealt with many people in crisis. On a sunny, hot day, I went into the room of a client. With the curtains still pulled shut, the bottom of my feet could be seen under the curtain. The person on the other side of the room greeted me with, "I know you are a Christian."

I proceeded to ask the client, "How do you know that I am Christian?"

The client informed me, "When you walked in the room, the Holy Spirit walked in the room with you."

Being new to the whole spiritual realm, I continued to speak with the client about his crisis. I should have asked the client how the Holy Spirit looked when he/she walked into the room with me.

On the West Coast, I traveled to many conferences. At one particular conference, the Holy Spirit continued to say, "Keep praying." I left my home in a rural environment in a very urban city. After entering the conference, the room was very cold and dark. All the people at the conference were hugging and telling one another how much they were in love with the Holy Spirit.

As I continued to pray, I went into the bathroom, and the Holy Spirit prompted me to leave the conference. Before I could leave the bathroom, a lady came up to me and said, "We are in love with the Holy Spirit. Why are you leaving the conference."

I decided to let the woman know that I was thinking about leaving and would stay a little longer. The Holy Spirit prompted me to leave the conference because the Spirit informed me that the type of love she was referring to was not of God. I left the conference early and made it back to my apartment complex safely.

On a cold fall day, I decided to go to a conference up by the Grand Canyon. The drive took me several hours. On the way, the Holy Spirit told me to watch out for deer while on the road. I did not pay any attention to the small voice. The area had a lot of grass that had a gold tint on top. I kept saying, "God is so beautiful to make such a unique color tone for the earth."

I tried to find the conference for over an hour. I saw a camp that looked like it was down a hill. So I drove up to the hill with the white tent. In the tent, I walked into a camp meeting that had a world-announced leader. She prophesied to all the people in the meeting. In the meeting, she let all the people know that their presence was due to a supernatural invitation. After she prayed for everyone, I met a couple of ladies at the snack area. We exchanged telephone numbers and prayed for one another's safe travels back home.

On my way home, it was very dark, without any street lights in the mountains. I continued to drive around the mountains. I heard the Holy Spirit say, "Be watchful." I turned up my music while driving at 11:00 p.m. in the mountains. After about an hour and a half of driving, I looked to my left and saw about five adult deer on the side of the road. I continued to pray that the deer would not cross the road because I didn't have an alternative lane to jump over into. I prayed and continued to drive all the way back home. The Holy Spirit kept the deer on the side of the road and allowed me to make it home safely. Around two in the morning, I received a call from a lady in the conference to ask me about making it home safely. She let me know that on her ride home, many moose met her on the side of the road. The lady told me, "I am glad that leader prayed for supernatural experiences over us because I know that is what got us home safely out of the mountains and those wild animals from crossing the road."

While traveling from the West Coast to the East Coast, I was able to walk into a convenience store that had a lot of random items. In the convenience store, I saw an aisle full of small angel and devil figurines on the shelf. I came across a picture of Jesus sitting at the table during the Last Supper. As most of the time, I didn't think anything much of the pictures or items seen through the store. I drove twenty hours prior to reaching Memphis, Tennessee. While in Memphis, I spent some time with my family. Some of my relatives took me out to eat for a special occasion. I kept hearing a small voice say, "Be careful which table you sit at."

While out at a popular restaurant in Memphis, Tennessee, I saw a set of national spiritual leaders eating at a table. As we left the restaurant, the Holy Spirit kept saying, "Be careful who you eat with." I continued to drive and had made it three hours from my destination when it started raining very heavily. The enemy always brings a storm to distract a servant leader from their destination. Again, I could not see while on the road. I kept praying, and less than a minute later, there was a sign that said, "Rest area next exit." The Holy Spirit will always provide an exit when the enemy brings a storm.

Devotion Day 5

The Education Journey
of a Servant Leader

While in grade school, I had to change schools because of my parents' divorce. I would have to catch up on work for several days while having to stay with my parents, who live in different households. With much hard work, I received a lot of honor roll certificates. In one class, a grade school teacher tried to make the class difficult. With a lot of hard work, I was able to continue to pass the class.

The enemy comes to disrupt a servant leader's education.

While in college, I conceived an untimely gift: a healthy baby boy. I received many comments from my peers and family that I would never be able to make it through college. What the devil meant for evil, God meant for good. It was a lot of work being a single parent while in college. I began my college journey working toward an early childhood degree to help single mothers have a safe environment for their children. After receiving my early childhood degree, I decided to start a new journey toward being a servant for people who were faced with oppression. I continued my journey and graduated with a degree to help people in the oppressed population.

While continuing my education, I entered into an accelerated program to receive support from oppressed populations in the community. In the program, the work was very fast and moved at a very quick pace. In the environment, I was faced with a lot of adversity while trying to finish the work while being a single parent. With much hard work and prayer, I would say that God allowed my son and me to continue our educational journey.

My son, who is an adult at this time, completed high school with honors. He was supported by all the faculty for his educational drive and artwork. The educators at his schools placed him in the top five of his class while on the West Coast.

When servant leaders are placed in untimely situations, God will give them the strength and courage to move forward with God's plan for their life.

After going to school for over twenty years, I had a professor tell us to write on social justice. I decided to write about the topic that God told me to write about. I wrote about police brutality toward women and minorities in March. I was informed by my professor that police brutality happens a lot of the time, and the subject was very basic. I told her that police brutality against oppressed populations should never be seen as basic. Two weeks later, the George Floyd case was televised throughout the country. I called the professor back and told her that a higher power told me to write the paper because the nature of oppressed populations being hurt on a regular basis should never be seen as a simple or normal issue in society.

The enemy will try to get a servant leader to question what the Holy Spirit has told the servant to discuss while saving people.

Devotion Day 6

The Different Works of
a Servant Leader

The servant leaders' mission is to be servants first. A servant chosen by God is not impressed with titles or positions. Servant leaders take on the role of leading people to safety. Servant leaders stand up to do what is right, even with the odds against them.

Women servant leaders face many layers of opposition while fulfilling their role to serve. Servant leaders see the oppression and obstacles as an opportunity for God to show people that He is real. While serving in an organization with people dealing with oppression, I heard the Holy Spirit tell me to talk about the closing of churches in September 2019. I received a lot of negative responses when I told leaders about God closing churches. As a little country girl from Millington, Tennessee, I didn't know that many people connected the closing of the church to money being missed.

God told me that when the people who are called by my name would turn from wicked ways, then I would open up the heavens and heal the land around them. I took the rejection from leaders and questioned what the Holy Spirit had told me about Him closing churches. The next year, COVID hit the nation, and many churches were closed because of the pandemic. Like the rest of the world, I never knew what a pandemic was at the time.

Devotion Day 7

The Traits of a Servant Leader in the Community

My father volunteered for the military at the young age of seventeen. While in the military, he served his country for several years. The military decided to send my father to Vietnam and place him on the front lines to fight in the war. In the war, my father got separated from his platoon for several days. While in the jungle, my father lost his leg. He continued to fight the enemy while in the jungle. The sergeants came to my grandmother's door and told her that my father had passed away. My grandmother looked the sergeants in the eyes and told them that the Holy Spirit had told her that my father was not dead and to go back to the jungle and get him. The soldiers went looking for my father and brought him back to the United States the next day. The power of the Holy Spirit through prayer has a way of telling us things through the supernatural realm.

The seven-day devotion is meant to let people know that the Holy Spirit is real and that other forces of darkness are real.

About the Author

Pamela Vann has been a servant in the community and in the church for over twenty years. She brings a host of knowledge and insight into the paths of serving as a leader. Born in Millington, Tennessee, in a small town outside of Memphis, she understood at an early age the power of God. Currently, Pamela works as an advocate to serve disenfranchised populations. She truly believes the world can and will become a better place when servants of God lead in their highest calling.